I Am in me

Reality

Leonardo (Leni) Gomez

ISBN 979-8-89243-039-5 (paperback)
ISBN 979-8-89243-040-1 (digital)

Christian Faith Publishing
832 Park Avenue
Meadville, PA 16335
www.christianfaithpublishing.com

Printed in the United States of America

If there's a scripture I would say exemplifies Leni, it would be this:

> *And Jesus came and spoke to them, saying, "All authority has been given to Me in heaven and on earth. Go therefore and make disciples of all the nations, baptizing them in the name of the Father and of the Son and of the Holy Spirit, teaching them to observe all things that I have commanded you; and lo, I am with you always, even to the end of the age." Amen. (Matthew 28:18–20 NKJV)*

Leni is a man who has a passion for the lost but not just for the lost to get saved. He has a passion for them to be discipled into the image of the Lord Jesus Christ. That is exactly what comes out in the book that he had just written. His goal in life is to see souls saved and developed. I'm asking you to read his book with an open heart and enjoy it as he ministers to you through it. What is written here is done out of a heart of love.

Pastor Darrell Morgan, Senior Pastor, "Word of Life Church," Apopka, Florida

CONTENTS

CONTENTS

Introduction

Father, I thank you for the opportunity to share Your love and Your reality with those reading this today. As they read each word, may there be an ever-increasing fire and desire for You. Reality of Jesus, come. Awaken them to the kingdom of God and the realm of His glory.

Father, I hear You saying to me, "Son, I have called you for such a time as this. As the person reading this discovers the story of your life in Me, they will receive a passion they have never known available. I will increase and stir them to live out all I have created them for. I Am directing every word and page. As we are one, our words will be one. Passion will increase, religion will fall away, and the ways of this world will be exposed as they learn Me in our relationship. I love you, son, and those reading this. Both you and the reader will increase in measures you have yet to experience." (He smiled when He said that.)

This book has come out of a life with God but from a person who didn't believe in a *God*. I also never wanted to be caught as a weak-minded, boring *Christian*. My life seemed fine to me. I had everything the world would say you need: money, roof over my head, custody of my child, girlfriends, car, etc. I definitely didn't want to waste my time in a church reading the Bible or being good. Still today, most of the examples we have of Christianity are boring and without life. This book will open your eyes to the reality of a Spirit-filled life in a relationship with an unseen God who is your Father.

Say this out loud, "Father, I receive all You have for me as I read this in Jesus's name."

Reality

I was leaning over my girlfriend one night. She was twitching and slightly convulsing. You see, we had been indulging in all types of drugs for over a year. This particular night wasn't out of the norm. However, as I leaned over her, I was thinking, *I really need to take her outside to the patio to get some air. She needs to stop, or I'm going to have to call 911.* As I was contemplating this, I felt someone walk behind me.

Strangely, in my apartment, it was just my girlfriend, myself, and two other girls in the room to my right just down the hallway. However, I felt the presence of a person walk behind me from my left side to my right. We had done several drugs and had experienced hallucinations frequently. I'm saying this because at this point in my life, hallucinations was a normal thing; however, tonight was different. I felt a presence walk by me.

As I felt that presence, I turned and looked to see who it was. I saw a man walking to the room where the other two girls were. In the doorway of that room was this large lady looking at me.

The truth is, that's the last thing I remember from that night. My girlfriend didn't die and was *fine*. We did not call 911. I don't recall what happened the rest of that night, but what I do recall is that there were people in my house I did not invite, and that bothered me. I really didn't believe in God, anything unseen, or a supernatural realm. I was my own boss. If I believed in anything, it was the power of positive thinking. Coincidentally, I was introduced to a realm that I knew nothing about, and I had people in my house that I did not invite.

I mentioned my girlfriend was *fine*, but within the week, she ended up in a psychiatric facility. I was still shaken by the uninvited *people* in my apartment, so I reached out to my older brother.

My dad died when I was a young teen, and all the family I had at this point in my life was my mom and brother. My brother was always a Christian. Christians believe in a God they can't see, so I figured he might know something about these *people*. I reached out and said, "Hey. I'm not sure what's going on, but there are people in my house that I did not invite."

After explaining what I meant, he turned me over to his pastor. The pastor gave me a call within twenty-four hours. When we spoke on the phone, he asked me to pray through my apartment out loud while he led me through what to pray. I agreed and started walking and praying, repeating what he would say. There were two areas where I struggled to speak or repeat the words of this pastor. In fact, I felt like I was being choked.

When we finished praying, he advised me, "Those areas you struggled to get the words out are most likely the areas of the highest activity of the sin you are into." Surprisingly, he didn't know where I was in the apartment because we were on the phone, and this was way before FaceTime. What he didn't know, and to my amazement, was how accurate he was. The bathroom, which is where I would cook the drugs, and the master bedroom were the areas I could not speak. I took this information in and was scared straight for about a week.

I didn't visit his church, but he did mail me a Bible. I share this with you because I didn't get saved, but it was an awakening to the possibility of something more than meets the eye. The possibility of an unseen realm around us.

Fast-forward to about a year later. I was now a single parent with custody of my son and, unfortunately, still on drugs. Due to my son not having his mother in his life and my brother now always asking me to come to church, I figured, *What the heck, let me kill two birds with one stone and take my son to church.* The churches are always full of women and are always teaching God is love. Maybe he can receive a side of love I cannot offer, and it will shut my brother up about coming to church. Wednesday nights became a thing. During the drive to church, I would smoke a joint with my son in the car since I didn't believe in God. Actually, this was my norm when I went anywhere.

I went to church for several months. Instead of just dropping my son off, I would sit in the service. I thought the people were crazy because although I was high, they seemed to be higher than me.

One day when I was getting ready for work, I thought, *I'm gonna stop going to church. Those people are crazy.* It only took seconds to think as I was getting dressed. I worked at a telemarketing room and dealt drugs to my coworkers. As I was sitting at my desk/cubicle, this lady approached me and said, "God told me to tell you something."

This caught me off guard because she sat at the other end of the office with two other ladies. They didn't like me. I knew this because I was constantly getting spoken to about my foul mouth due to them. When she stated God told her to tell me something, I immediately thought, *Weed, I have. Cocaine, I have, but this lady needs lithium. She is hearing voices.* I looked at her skeptically and jeered, "Okay, what did God tell you?"

"God told me to tell you not to quit. He will be with you. He will be by your side," she replied and quietly walked away. Confronted with the fact this *God* could hear my thoughts, I slowly turned into my cubicle, bothered, and thought, *All right, God, I'm gonna find out who You are. I don't want to know who my brother or the pastor or anybody says You are. I want to find out who You are so when I find You and turn from You, I can say I turned from God and not church.*

Many people go to church, get hurt, and stop going but never actually make contact with God. I just realized that there's a God that can hear my thoughts, and if He can hear my thoughts, then He can be found. Consequently, I made a quest at that moment to find God for myself. Not to be a Christian but to spit on Him and say I didn't need Him. I had an attitude and wanted to prove I could survive on my own since I had been doing it from my early teens after my dad died.

On April 29, 1996, I was on a lunch break at a new job. I'd been going to church, seeking God, reading, praying, doing everything I was taught to reach God. At this point I had just come off a great weekend at church with God, thinking I heard Him say to me, *If you get rid of your worldly high, I will give you My spiritual high.*

On my break, I was going to pick up a quarter pound of weed. I still needed to sell and make money because I was a single parent. After picking up this quarter pound, I got in the only car accident I've been in. It happened in slow motion. I rear-ended someone, then someone rear-ended me.

4

I got out of my car. The front and rear ends were both smashed, I had weed in the car, and the cops were on the way. As I stood there on the side of the road, I turned my attention to the Lord, and I said in a matter-of-fact way, "You want my life, You can have it. But Your Word says that if I seek first Your kingdom and Your righteousness, all these things will be added on to me. Let me see what You can do."

That was the day I surrendered my life to the Lord. From that moment on, I can share with you, story after story, how God has taken care of me. His word is true, and He is looking for someone to hold Him accountable to it so He can show forth His goodness. Keep in mind, I wanted to find Him to spit on Him and say, "I don't need You." However, He overlooked my stupidity and showed me love. I had been longing for something and filling my life with the world trying to find it. It was Him I was looking for.

He came in, and everything just fell off of me. I was made new. I felt new. I saw new. I spoke new.

> *Now, if anyone is enfolded into Christ, he has become an entirely new person. All that is related to the old order has vanished. Behold, everything is fresh and new. (2 Corinthians 5:17 TPT)*

God is actually real. For the first six months of my salvation, I continually wept. I would look at people, Christian or not, and tell them, "He's real. He is actually real." God became real to me. Through this book, you will see glimpses of reality that will inspire you and light a fire in you to know and live for Him.

What the Heck Happened to Me?

Oh no! I had become a *Christian*. Yikes! Something I vowed I'd never be. In the last chapter, you read how I was not the best candidate for *Christianity*. Drugs had only been a small portion of my issues. At the point of writing this book, I have less friends from that time that are free and alive. Most of the guys I used to hang out with are either dead or serving time.

Anyway, did I mention I live in Florida? Oh yeah, beautiful Florida. The beach is an hour east to the Atlantic and two hours west to the Gulf. I grew up and graduated high school in Orlando. Anyone familiar with the school system around here knows education isn't one of the attractions. My reading level, or the extent of my reading, was CD inserts.

Why am I saying this? I never wanted to be a Christian. Christianity was presented to me in a package I did not want or care to even try. This was the *pitch*: go to church, read the Bible, and be good. Go to church? *Out*. Not giving up half my weekend to sit around with a bunch of squares. No, thank you. Read the Bible? *Next*. Be good? Are you kidding me? The only thing I was good at was not getting caught. Those three things were the reason Christianity had no appeal to me.

So what the heck happened to me? I mean, something happened that day on the side of the road, on April 29, 1996. I had become a different person. Like I was struck by lightning or possibly filled with light. I was changed, made new. No more drugs, and I didn't have to go through rehab. I was clean. I did not curse anymore; it just left me. I didn't even have to try. My outside looked the same, although someone said I looked different. However, I was brand-new from the inside.

Something happened inside of me. It's probably best if I described it like this. Let's say I placed you on an operating table, unconscious. While you're on the table, I equipped your entire body from head to toe with bionics.

While you are now fully bionic, I wake you up, and I say, "Hi! I made some changes to you. Take this tennis ball, and I'd like you to throw it. Remember, you are different, so have faith the outcome will be different than before."

You look at me, you look at the ball, and then you throw it. The ball goes for miles. Your eyes get wide, and you look at me like you've seen a ghost. You're like, "Oh my goodness. What is going on? What did you do to me? I still look the same and kinda feel the same but…"

Then I'm like, "Oh yeah!" I hand you this instruction book (the Bible). "This will teach you about what's going on inside of you. Come over on Friday nights or Sunday mornings (church), and we can share other things we found in the manual. Philip, someone who is born-again (bionic), discovered time travel."

Jesus answered, "Nicodemus, listen to this eternal truth: Before a person can even perceive

7

God's kingdom, they must first experience a rebirth." (John 3:3 TPT)

Now, if anyone is enfolded into Christ, he has become an entirely new person. All that is related to the old order has vanished. Behold, everything is fresh and new. (2 Corinthians 5:17 TPT)

His passion is to remain true to the Word of "I AM," meditating day and night on the true revelation of light. (Psalm 1:2 TPT)

Stop imitating the ideals and opinions of the culture around you, but be inwardly transformed by the Holy Spirit through a total reformation of how you think. This will empower you to discern God's will as you live a beautiful life, satisfying and perfect in his eyes. (Romans 12:2 TPT)

And he has appointed some with grace to be apostles, and some with grace to be prophets, and some with grace to be evangelists, and some with grace to be pastors, and some with grace to be teachers. And their calling is to nurture and prepare all the holy believers to do their own works of ministry, and as they do this they will enlarge and build up the body of Christ. These grace ministries will function until we all attain oneness into the faith, until we all experience the fullness of what it means to know the Son of God, and finally we become one into a perfect man with the full dimensions of spiritual maturity and fully developed into the abundance of Christ. (Ephesians 4:11–13 TPT)

It takes a grinding wheel to sharpen a blade, and so one person sharpens the character of another. (Proverbs 27:17 TPT)

"As for being good, my friend, if you are fully bionic / born-again, why would you go outside of your new nature?"

Therefore if any person is [ingrafted] in Christ (the Messiah) he is a new creation (a new creature altogether); the old [previous moral and spiritual condition] has passed away. Behold, the fresh and new has come! (2 Corinthians 5:17 AMPC)

And I will ask the Father and he will give you another Savior, the Holy Spirit of Truth, who will be to you a friend just like me— and he will never leave you. The world won't receive him because they can't see him or know him. But you know him intimately because he remains with you and will live inside you." *(John 14:16–17 TPT)*

But now, independently of the law, the righteousness of God is tangible and brought to light through Jesus, the Anointed One. This is the righteousness that the Scriptures prophesied would come. It is God's righteousness made visible through the faithfulness of Jesus Christ. And now all who believe in him receive that gift. For there is really no difference between us, for we all have sinned and are in need of the glory of God. Yet through his powerful declaration of acquittal, God freely gives away his righteousness. His gift of love and favor now cascades over us, all because Jesus, the Anointed One, has liberated us from the guilt, punishment, and power of sin! (Romans 3:21–24 TPT)

That's what happened to me! I'm not a person that wants to be good or go to church. I am a son of God with the Spirit of God dwelling in this body. I realized that I had worked pretty hard for the enemy in my old body. As a new creation in Christ, I would now commit to not just sit around on a Sunday morning and call myself a Christian. It was time to let everyone know what had happened to me and the truth of His reality.

When given an opportunity to write a recommendation for this book, I thought, "This will be easy." Why would I say that? Well, in the years I have known Leni, I have been seeing Colossians 1:27 manifested in him.

> **To them God willed to make known what are the riches of the glory of this mystery among the Gentiles: which is Christ in you, the hope of glory. (Colossians 1:27 NKJV)**

Each year I see more of Jesus manifested in Leni than I did the year before. Leni did not just write some principles or laws to follow. No, he wrote about what the living GOD of creation has done in him and through him. He is fully convinced that our Father wants to do the same with every person who calls upon the name of Jesus. *I Am in me* is a great tool for the kingdom. It will be used to bring people to salvation. It will bring believers to a more intimate fellowship with our Father.

Pastor Frank Mangialomini

Have you forgotten that your body is now the sacred temple of the Spirit of Holiness, who lives in you? You don't belong to yourself any longer, for the gift of God, the Holy Spirit, lives inside your sanctuary. (1 Corinthians 6:19 TPT)

Son

Worship was amazing!

I was taking a vacation with the Lord and visiting a conference outside the US. As a new creation and now a son of God, I would find ways to spend time with Him. This particular time was pivotal for me in my relationship with Him.

Worship had ended, and I was headed back to my seat. Overflowing with joy and gladness, I wanted to share my delight with others. I had met some new friends at this conference and figured I would share a picture of my son with them. I had a picture of Lennie with a tie on for his school picture in the front of my Bible.

I went to my seat to grab my Bible, and as I did, I was taken into a vision. I can't really explain what happened. The only thing I can say is what I saw and felt. In this vision, there were three men gathered around the Lord, all looking at something. When I approached to look over their shoulders, I saw the Lord's hand. On His palm was a picture of me. Exactly what I was wanting to do with my son, He was doing with me in heaven. It absolutely wrecked me. I sobbed like a baby.

You see, my dad died a week before I turned fourteen. From that point on, I became my own boss. I lived with the guilt of his death until I saw my Father in heaven boasting about me. When I was sobbing, He was talking to me about how He had always desired to father me.

> *Jesus explained, "I am the Way, I am the*
> *Truth, and I am the Life. No one comes next to*
> *the Father except through union with me. To*
> *know me is to know my Father too." (John 14:6*
> *TPT)*

God has always wanted to father us, and Jesus is the door that opens that relationship back up. "Back up?" you ask. Yes! Let's look at the beginning,

> *And in love he chose us before he laid the*
> *foundation of the universe! Because of his great*
> *love, he ordained us, so that we would be seen*
> *as holy in his eyes with an unstained innocence.*
> *(Ephesians 1:4 TPT)*

This means before He spoke the universe into existence, He chose us. How is this possible? I know Christianity and the Bible does not teach reincarnation; however, there are scriptures that do teach us about our thoughts and imaginations.

> *But I say to you that everyone who so*
> *much as looks at a woman with evil desire for*
> *her has already committed adultery with her in*
> *his heart. (Matthew 5:28 AMPC)*

I don't see any spoken or physical action here. How about this one?

> *We can demolish every deceptive fantasy*
> *that opposes God and break through every*
> *arrogant attitude that is raised up in defiance*
> *of the true knowledge of God. We capture, like*
> *prisoners of war, every thought and insist that*
> *it bow in obedience to the Anointed One. (2*
> *Corinthians 10:5 TPT)*

What does that mean, "to capture your thoughts like a prisoner"? There is clearly more to our thoughts and meditations than meets the eye because we also have these instructions.

> *Yes, feast on all the treasures of the heav-*
> *enly realm and fill your thoughts with heavenly*
> *realities, and not with the distractions of the*
> *natural realm. (Colossians 3:2 TPT)*

Fill my thoughts?

> *This Book of the Law shall not depart out*
> *of your mouth, but you shall meditate on it day*
> *and night, that you may observe and do accord-*
> *ing to all that is written in it. For then you shall*
> *make your way prosperous, and then you shall*

deal wisely and have good success. (Joshua 1:8 AMPC)

This scripture says to meditate on the Word of God to be able to accomplish all it says.

I think you get the picture. God falls in love with us, creates a place for us (the universe), like He created the garden for Adam, so He can hang out with us. He creates us in His image so He has someone to be in relationship with that isn't different to Him like the animals.

Go with me here, and I will list the scriptures as well. He created Adam, and then after the animals, He created Eve from Adam. Adam couldn't fellowship with the animals, so He made Eve from Adam so they could relate to each other.

> *So God created man in His own image, in the image and likeness of God He created him; male and female He created them. (Genesis 1:27 AMPC)*

> *Then the Lord God formed man from the dust of the ground and breathed into his nostrils the breath or spirit of life, and man became a living being. (Genesis 2:7 AMPC)*

Sidenote here. You see, the breath of God is the Spirit of life birthing Adam out of the earth and then the woman from the man.

We see this happen in the book of Luke when Jesus is birthed by the Holy Spirit of God from the woman.

> *And the angel answered and said to her,*
> *"The Holy Spirit will come upon you, and*
> *the power of the Highest will overshadow you;*
> *therefore, also, that Holy One who is to be born*
> *will be called the Son of God." (Luke 1:35*
> *NKJV)*

The same Holy Spirit, or breath of God, created Adam and Jesus.

> *And the Lord God caused a deep sleep to*
> *fall upon Adam; and while he slept, He took*
> *one of his ribs or a part of his side and closed*
> *up the [place with] flesh. And the rib or part of*
> *his side which the Lord God had taken from the*
> *man He built up and made into a woman, and*
> *He brought her to the man. (Genesis 2:21–22*
> *AMPC)*

God desired to father us, be with us, and for us to carry on this earth as His sons and daughters. Look how close His relationship was with Adam. Adam named the animals.

Everything we do as parents, we do for our children, including anything we invent or create. With this in mind, think about how much love you have for your child. That love causes you to bring what you created to him or her and allow them to name it.

> *And Adam gave names to all the livestock*
> *and to the birds of the air and to every [wild]*
> *beast of the field; but for Adam there was not*
> *found a helper meet (suitable, adapted, com-*
> *plementary) for him. (Genesis 2:20 AMPC)*

Did you see that? Adam named the animals for himself! I just imagine God the Father bringing an object over to Adam and unveiling it. Adam looks at it with those big eyes your child gets when you give them a new toy. Adam says, "Elephant!"

Dad smiles and says, "Yes, son, elephant." Now that's an awesome dad!

He wants to father you; if you have never looked at Him as your Father, do it now. You are saved by grace through faith, not by works. You are not just saved to go to heaven. You are born again, saved by the blood of Jesus to restore what the enemy stole in the garden.

> *But of the tree of the knowledge of good*
> *and evil and blessing and calamity you shall*
> *not eat, for on the day that you eat of it you*
> *shall surely die. (Genesis 2:17 AMPC)*

> *But the serpent said to the woman, "You*
> *shall not surely die." But the Lord God called*

to Adam and said to him, "Where are you?"
(Genesis 3:4, 9 AMPC)

It was not physical death but spiritual death leading to a broken relationship and fellowship with Father God.

For our sake He made Christ [virtually] to be sin Who knew no sin, so that in and through Him we might become [endued with, viewed as being in, and examples of] the righteousness of God [what we ought to be, approved and acceptable and in right relationship with Him, by His goodness]. (2 Corinthians 5:21 AMPC)

Thus it is written, "The first man Adam became a living being (an individual personality); the last Adam (Christ) became a life-giving Spirit [restoring the dead to life]." (1 Corinthians 15:45 AMPC)

Jesus restored us to life. He restored our spirit beings so we can interact with Dad. Jesus took the stench of sin away from us so Father God can come close as we come close to Him. He is so good, so wonderful.

Oh, I forgot to list this scripture. The interesting thing is that when I saw my picture on His palm, I had no scripture reference for it. However, He is faithful. His Word is true, and He always confirms it.

> *Behold, I have indelibly imprinted (tattooed a picture of) you on the palm of each of My hands; [O Zion] your walls are continually before Me. (Isaiah 49:16 AMPC)*

As you read this book, I hope you can now see the perception in which this book is written: as a son of God in full trust and faith in his Father.

Trust

Let me ask you a question. If you were to walk over to the light switch and turn it on, how much faith or trust are you using that it will turn on when you hit the switch? How about the faucet or toilet? I mean, is there any doubt they will work or do what they were intended to do?

> *But when Jesus saw it, he was indignant and said to them, "Let the children come to me; do not hinder them, for to such belongs the kingdom of God. Truly, I say to you, whoever does not receive the kingdom of God like a child shall not enter it." (Mark 10:14–15 ESV)*

I was living in a two-bedroom duplex with my son. I'd been walking with God for a couple years when I came across this scripture. When I read it, I questioned what it meant "to be like a child in order to enter God's kingdom." I know it's by grace through faith that I am saved, but what is this about? I asked the Lord what it meant.

He answered with the question I posed above but of my son who was sleeping in his room. He asked, "Do you think when your son gets up in the middle of the night to go to the bathroom, he has any doubt the light will turn on or the toilet will flush?"

I replied, "No, that would not be normal for him to even question it."

Then He said to me, "That is the faith and trust in Me I want My children to have."

My son was around nine years old at that point. He knew his dad was good and took care of him, so he didn't have to wonder if the light switch worked. He simply knew it would work.

This is how our Father wants us all to live. In full trust that He is who He says He is. That His Word is true, never fails, and will never perish.

> *Sky and earth will pass away, but My words*
> *will not pass away. (Matthew 24:35 AMPC)*

He is not a man, who would lie.

> *God is not man, that he should lie, or a son*
> *of man, that he should change his mind. Has he*
> *said, and will he not do it? Or has he spoken,*
> *and will he not fulfill it? (Numbers 23:19 ESV)*

Do you trust Him? Having faith like a child—or as some say, childlike faith—is teachable, humbling, and trusting.

> *Whoever will humble himself therefore*
> *and become like this little child [trusting, lowly,*
> *loving, forgiving] is greatest in the kingdom of*
> *heaven. (Matthew 18:4 AMPC)*

I will ask you again, Do you trust Him? Well, let's see. I have counseled with many people, and when they come to me and say, "I'm just not like you" or "I don't get it," I want to be on fire. I read the Bible, and I go to church, but I keep going up and down with my walk. When I hear someone say this to me, my first question is, "How's your tithing?"

Oh, wait. Why are you bringing this up? I covered how God wanted to father me. Also how I'm living as a son with childlike faith—so yes, tithing. I'm not here to convince you whether it's of the Old Testament or New Testament, law or before the law. The truth is, your trust level with Dad will dictate how you will approach those scriptures.

Let's look back at when I was getting high on the way to church before I was saved. Wednesday nights, I would take Lennie to church. I believe they had a program called Royal Rangers for the kids, while I would sit in the service. At this point of my life, I had realized that there was good and evil, light and darkness, God and the devil.

My friend was a DJ downtown, and Wednesday nights were the nights he was featured. After service, I dropped Lennie off at his *abuela*'s and would go party downtown. During service, they would pass this bucket around for tithe and offering. In that time of my life, I only dealt with cash—no credit, no checks. What I had on me was what I had to my name. I never lacked, but I didn't own anything either. So the bucket would come my way, and I would take my money out of my pocket, split it in half, and place half of it in the bucket. My thought process was, *I will give half to God now since I am going to spend the other half on the devil later.*

That's what I did. What I noticed, however, was the change in my life. I was not born-again yet, although I had tapped into something that works in the natural realm as well as the spiritual. Opportunities started to open up to me. I started having more than just enough. It made no sense to me because I was a hood with long hair, a dealer on drugs, and I could barely read.

All of a sudden, I went from slinging drugs and stealing to a career that would eventually be the six-figure income I walked away from to work for my Father. I didn't know Scripture at the time I started to give. When I encountered a God who could hear my thoughts, I started to read, pray, and pay attention at church, and I ran into a scripture that puzzled me.

Remember, I surrendered my life to God on the side of the road, quoting Matthew 6:33. Just before, I read this:

> *No one can serve two masters; for either he will hate the one and love the other, or he will stand by and be devoted to the one and despise and be against the other. You cannot serve God and mammon (deceitful riches, money, possessions, or whatever is trusted in). (Matthew 6:24 AMPC)*

I read that and decided there was clearly a typo. It should say God or the devil, God or Lucifer, God or Satan; but no, it says God or money. Yikes! That's a big deal because most of us would not even consider worshipping the devil. I mean, he isn't even a god. He is a fallen angel.

You see, this is showing you that where your trust is, that is what you worship. Worship is from the heart, not lip service.

> *These people honor me only with their words, for their hearts are so very distant from me. (Matthew 15:8 TPT)*

How do you know if you are just offering lip service and your heart is far from the Lord? Let's go back to Matthew Chapter 6, just before he tells you, "You can't serve God or money." He says,

> *For where your treasure is, there will be your heart also. (Matthew 6:21 AMPC)*

Trusting God is faith in God, and 99.9 percent of the time, when someone is struggling with staying on fire with God, backsliding, or not understanding God in their life, I ask, "How is your tithing?"

They don't tithe or only do when they can. Both instances are a lack of trust in your Father. Let me tell you about my Dad.

> *I was once inexperienced, but now I'm old. Not once have I found a lover of God forsaken by him, nor have any of their children gone hungry. (Psalm 37:25 TPT)*

> *Who else has held the oceans in his hand? Who has measured off the heavens with his fin-*

gers? Who else knows the weight of the earth or has weighed the mountains and hills on a scale? (Isaiah 40:12 NLT)

He determines and counts the number of the stars; He calls them all by their names. (Psalm 147:4 AMPC)

And my God will liberally supply (fill to the full) your every need according to His riches in glory in Christ Jesus. (Philippians 4:19 AMPC)

Now that's my Dad! Who shall supply? My God! According to my performance? Nope! According to His riches and glory.

I was able to walk away from a six-figure career in order to work directly for my Father because I've always trusted Him. Funny thing is that after I surrendered my life on April 29, 1996, I would hear or would read the "tithing scriptures," and they say, "Give a tenth." Ha! I guess when you start with half, a tenth is nothing.

Giving is God's nature. He gave His Son to reap sons and daughters. Sowing and reaping. You want to be blessed every day? Then sow every day. The return on a seed is much greater than the seed. Look at the five thousand men plus women and children who were fed.

But all we have is five barley loaves and two fish. (Matthew 14:17 TPT)

> *And everyone ate until they were satisfied,*
> *for the food was multiplied in front of their*
> *eyes! They picked up the leftovers and filled up*
> *twelve baskets full! There were about five thou-*
> *sand men who were fed, in addition to many*
> *women and children! (Matthew 14:20–21*
> *TPT)*

Someone had to give the five loaves and two fish to reap over five thousand men plus women and children being fed. They could have held on to what they had and not given it to Jesus. What, then, would have happened? Are you holding onto things thinking you need them? Trust God and see what happens. Let's not forget, after they had all eaten, they picked up twelve baskets full of leftovers. Does that even make sense?

> *And the very hairs on your head are all*
> *numbered. So don't be afraid; you are more*
> *valuable to God than a whole flock of spar-*
> *rows. (Luke 12:7 NLT)*

He knows the exact number of hairs on your head, and instead of multiplying the bread and fish exactly to all being fed, he supplied extra. Because He is a God of more than enough, El Shaddai. He is a good God, a good Father.

Let's look at how little He is concerned with money. Who carried the money for the disciples? Judas. Why on earth would you give your money or place your money in a bank that is owned by embezzlers and betrayers? Jesus did. Do you know more than Him?

I think He was showing us something. Let's be real, wouldn't more money in Jesus's treasury have helped Him get the message out? Look what happened to the person who had access to the treasury.

> *Do not love or cherish the world or the things that are in the world. If anyone loves the world, love for the Father is not in him. (1 John 2:15 AMPC)*

> *Loving money is a root of all evils. Some people run after it so much that they have given up their faith. Craving more money pushes them away from the faith into error, compounding misery in their lives! (1 Timothy 6:10 TPT)*

So again I ask, what are you trusting in? God or money? I found one of the only places that God says you can test Him.

> *"Bring all the tithes into the storehouse so there will be enough food in my Temple. If you do," says the Lord of Heaven's Armies, "I will open the windows of heaven for you. I will pour out a blessing so great you won't have enough room to take it in! Try it! Put me to the test!" (Malachi 3:10 NLT)*

He is good. You can trust Him!

> *Every gift God freely gives us is good and perfect, streaming down from the Father of lights, who shines from the heavens with no hidden shadow or darkness and is never subject to change. (James 1:17 TPT)*

Intimacy

Are you going through anything? Is your marriage okay? How are your finances? Are you dealing with sickness, anxiety, or depression? Are you on medication? Think about whatever it is you are going through.

Meditate on this. What if Jesus Christ of Nazareth knocked on your door right now? You answer the door in shock and amazement, maybe fall to your knees. He picks you up and says, "You get Me for the next two weeks."

For the next two weeks, the Jesus of the Bible (you know, the one who walked on water, calmed the storm, healed the sick, multiplied food, sent Peter to get money out of a fish, didn't condemn the woman in adultery) is your best buddy. He is with you, by your side, for everything—sitting on the couch, reading bedtime (hope you give Him the better bed), breakfast, lunch, dinner, TV time, bathroom (He is not looking), shower (again, not looking); He is by your side. He is at your house with you for two weeks!

As you meditate on Him physically being with you, how would the issues mentioned above be in your life? Do you think any of the current issues you are dealing with would still be there if Jesus was physically there? Have you meditated and taken Him through your day on what that could look like?

Not a lot to eat here—done! All the food you had in the fridge and in the pantry now multiplied with more than enough. Bank account is low, He informs you how to get more out of your current job or to look on the other side of the street for a new one. Head hurts, anxiety, depression, need meds—nope! You give it to Him. He looks at you with compassion and says, "Healed."

You pick up your phone to scroll on something sinful and realize He is right there. He looks at you and says, "I don't condemn you. Go and sin no more."

Life would be different, wouldn't it? Man, Jesus with me for two weeks! Life would be different for sure! Take a look at what Jesus says to the disciples.

> *But now I am going to Him Who sent Me, yet none of you asks Me, "Where are You going?" But because I have said these things to you, sorrow has filled your hearts [taken complete possession of them]. However, I am telling you nothing but the truth when I say it is profitable (good, expedient, advantageous) for you that I go away. Because if I do not go away, the Comforter (Counselor, Helper, Advocate, Intercessor, Strengthener, Standby) will not come to you [into close fellowship with you]; but if I go away, I will send Him to you [to be in close fellowship with you]. (John 16:5–7 AMPC)*

Jesus says its better if He physically leaves so that the Holy Spirit can come because physically He can only be in one place at one time but now Dad is sending His Spirit to be in fellowship with us each all the time. Remember Jesus said this a couple chapters prior.

> *But the Comforter (Counselor, Helper, Intercessor, Advocate, Strengthener, Standby), the Holy Spirit, Whom the Father will send in My name [in My place, to represent Me and act on My behalf], He will teach you all things. And He will cause you to recall (will remind you of, bring to your remembrance) everything I have told you. (John 14:26 AMPC)*

Thank You, Jesus!

How real is He to you? Because to the measure you actually believe He is real and with you is the measure to which you will live this life *in Him*.

We have already addressed that if He was physically at your house, things would probably be different. The Scripture explains it is now possible for Him to be with you at your house.

You see, we all believe that we accept Jesus into our hearts, yet we only acknowledge Him on Sunday when we visit a building called *church*. In Scripture, Jesus tells a woman something that can be taken as a foreshadow of what He was rearranging in this process of worshipping, acknowledging, and spending time with God.

> *Believe me, dear woman, the time has come when you will worship the Father neither on a mountain nor in Jerusalem, but in your heart. From now on, worshiping the Father will not be a matter of the right place but with a right heart. For God is a Spirit, and he longs to have sincere worshipers who adore him in the realm of the Spirit and in truth. (John 4:21, 23–24 TPT)*

Amplified adds "reality."

> *A time will come, however, indeed it is already here, when the true (genuine) worshipers will worship the Father in spirit and in truth (reality); for the Father is seeking just such people as these as His worshipers. (John 4:23 AMPC)*

Going to church is great, but having God with you all the time, twenty-four seven, is life-changing.

"How can I make God more real to me?" is the question I asked myself years ago. I had to do something to help my carnal self realize He is always with me. I worked at a job that involved a lot of windshield time.

I was determined to have the Lord ride with me every time I was in the car. I would have the passenger seat cleared off for Him. I didn't have to do this, but I did have to do this because my flesh needed to recognize He was there. So from there on, and even sometimes to this day, I clear off the seat; and if there is anything on there, I take it off and apologize.

How real is He to you? This is how I was able to train my body to recognize He is always there. You can have constant communication with Him.

> *Always be joyful. Never stop praying. Be thankful in all circumstances, for this is God's will for you who belong to Christ Jesus. (1 Thessalonians 5:16–18 NLT)*

How joyful and thankful would you live if your body was trained to recognize Him all the time? This is what I did to shift my salvation to a fellowship with Him at all times.

Let's look at how God views our lives. Most people believe that when they receive Jesus, they obtain a golden ticket so that when they die, they will go to heaven. It is frequently believed we are here on this earth to just make it through, and in death, we would have victory because we now go to heaven.

Odd thought, isn't it? Looking forward to death. Is that what you think our heavenly Father wants? To just barely make it through this life even though He gives us His Spirit? However, God says it's a close relationship.

Remember He says in John, "I am the way the truth and the life no one comes to the father but through me." Jesus opens the door to the relationship. Although, how do you know it's for now? He said this a little earlier in the book of John:

> *I speak to you an eternal truth: if you embrace my message and believe in the One who sent me, you will never face condemnation. In me, you have already passed from the realm of death into eternal life! (John 5:24 TPT)*

An eternal truth means even when time no longer exists, this fact will. What fact or truth is that? When you receive Jesus, you become an eternal being. Your spirit man is now everlasting. When you breathe your last breath, you exchange tents:

> *For we know that when this earthly tent we live in is taken down (that is, when we die and leave this earthly body), we will have a house in heaven, an eternal body made for us by God himself and not by human hands. We grow weary in our present bodies, and we long to put on our heavenly bodies like new cloth- ing. For we will put on heavenly bodies; we will not be spirits without bodies. (2 Corinthians 5:1–3 NLT)*

Your spirit is eternal now, and you can live and have intimacy with God from your spirit, but your earthly tent needs to be trained.

Let's look at an example the Lord gives us to help our understanding of intimacy with Him. He equates our life in Him to a marriage.

> *For the husband is head of the wife as*
> *Christ is the Head of the church, Himself the*
> *Savior of [His] body. (Ephesians 5:23 AMPC)*

We do believe He is the head and we are the body. The illustration He uses is a husband-and-wife kind of life, though.

> *For this reason a man shall leave his*
> *father and his mother and shall be joined to*
> *his wife, and the two shall become one flesh.*
> *[Gen. 2:24.] This mystery is very great, but I*
> *speak concerning [the relation of] Christ and*
> *the church. (Ephesians 5:31–32 AMPC)*

You are the church, His body. You are one with Him in a marriage-type relationship. Let's look at marriage and ways you fellowship with your spouse. With your loved one, you might go to the store, go out to eat, or go watch a movie. Out in public, but still together, communicating and fellowshipping. Then there are date nights where it's just the two of you. The conversation time is more intimate; however, there is always communication, even when things aren't said.

If you have been married for a while or even known someone for a long time, you might know what they will say before they say it.

Why? Because of the time you have spent together. It's the same way with the Lord. The more you acknowledge Him in all circumstances (car, store, date night), the more you get to know each other.

Have your parents ever mentioned the old sayings, "Show me your friends, and I'll show you your future," or "You are whom you hang around"? Well, guess what? You can hang out with the Lord all the time and become more like Him, like the scripture says.

> *In this [union and communion with Him] love is brought to completion and attains perfection with us, that we may have confidence for the day of judgment [with assurance and boldness to face Him], because as He is, so are we in this world. (1 John 4:17 AMPC)*

In this world, you can be like Jesus. If we spent more time with Him and in His Word, because Jesus is the Word, we wouldn't have to worry about sinning. You become what you focus on, so don't focus on not sinning, because Jesus already defeated the power of sin and death. Focus on and spend time with the Lord.

I live by a college, and on any given day, there will be a female jogging on the sidewalk while I am driving. My attention to her or lack of attention to her is a direct reflection of my time, fellowship, and intimacy with my wife. You see, if I'm passionately in love with my wife (I'll get back to that), and our communication, fellowship, and intimacy is good, then, like Jesus said, "the world has nothing in me." I don't even see the girl. The key to living clean isn't focusing on right or wrong, like in the garden. It is focusing on the walks with God in the cool of the day.

Let's address "passionately in love with my wife." The Scriptures say to love God first and your neighbor as yourself. When you speak to most Christians, they will say they love God; but talk to them long enough, and they will say they love Mexican food or coffee with the same emphasis. They love those but will tell you the next day they love Italian food or speed drinks. Either way, they throw the word *love* out there but really aren't devoted to it.

I enjoy reading the passion translation, because look how this reads:

> *Jesus answered him, "Love the Lord your God with every passion of your heart, with all the energy of your being, and with every thought that is within you." (Matthew 22:37 TPT)*

"Every passion of your heart." Ask my wife how annoying I can be at times because I constantly seek her attention. You see, when you are *in* love, you will think about and talk to the one who has your heart.

When you wake up, they are the first to hear you address them with good morning. When you are out driving, they are there in the seat next to you, or you are texting and calling them. Why? Because you are *in* love, always thinking of them and wanting to be with them.

That's what I'm talking about. Fall in love with God, and you are like, "Good morning, Lord. What would You like to do today? How are You doing?" The conversation is always available and open.

I pray this has opened your eyes and heart to have an open fellowship with the Lord every waking moment of your day. You will have that changed life we discussed if He came home with you for two weeks. Enjoy!

Oh, and it's okay if you don't have this passion for the Lord currently. Simply turn your attention to Him right now and say, "Help me, Lord. Help me fall deeper in love with You and Your Word. Give me a passion for You and a reality that You are always here and available for me. Thank You, Jesus!"

I Am in me

Little children, you are of God [you belong to Him] and have [already] defeated and overcome them [the agents of the antichrist], because He Who lives in you is greater (mightier) than he who is in the world. (1 John 4:4 AMPC)

Little children, you can be certain that you belong to God and have conquered them, for the One who is living in you is far greater than the one who is in the world. (1 John 4:4 TPT)

Where does God live now? In you! God prophesied it under the Old Testament and old covenant (OT/OC):

And I will put my Spirit within you and cause you to walk in My statutes, and you shall heed My ordinances and do them. (Ezekiel 36:27 AMPC)

Then you see Jesus says:

> *Loving me empowers you to obey my commands. And I will ask the Father and he will give you another Savior, the Holy Spirit of Truth, who will be to you a friend just like me—and he will never leave you. The world won't receive him because they can't see him or know him. But you know him intimately because he remains with you and will live inside you. (John 14:15–17 TPT)*

> *Jesus replied, "Loving me empowers you to obey my word. And my Father will love you so deeply that we will come to you and make you our dwelling place." (John 14:23 TPT)*

Read that again and meditate on it for a bit. Where does God live in the life of a born-again disciple of Christ Jesus? Look what Paul says:

> *Have you forgotten that your body is now the sacred temple of the Spirit of Holiness, who lives in you? You don't belong to yourself any longer, for the gift of God, the Holy Spirit, lives inside your sanctuary. (1 Corinthians 6:19 TPT)*

He refers to your body as a temple of God, which makes you a carrier of the Holy One. Now that is a seriously awesome thing. Look at the OT/OC and where God made His home: the ark of the covenant. I mean, how big of a deal was this? Take a look at this example; however, you should do a study of the temple and ark when you have a chance.

> *And David and all Israel were celebrating before God with all their might, with song and lyres and harps and tambourines and cymbals and trumpets. And when they came to the threshing floor of Chidon, Uzzah put out his hand to take hold of the ark, for the oxen stumbled. And the anger of the Lord was kindled against Uzzah, and he struck him down because he put out his hand to the ark, and he died there before God. (1 Chronicles 13:8–10 ESV)*

The ark was a big deal, I would say. They were praising God, and Uzzah was doing what seemed to be a good deed by steadying the ark. However, he died. That's pretty serious!

Can you think of a time in the New Testament or new covenant (NT/NC) where something similar happened? The believers were in *church* giving *good deeds*, but according to Peter, someone lied to the

Holy Spirit. Where was the Holy Spirit that He could be lied to? In Peter:

> *But a man named Ananias, with his wife Sapphira, sold a piece of property, and with his wife's knowledge he kept back for himself some of the proceeds and brought only a part of it and laid it at the apostles' feet. But Peter said, "Ananias, why has Satan filled your heart to lie to the Holy Spirit and to keep back for yourself part of the proceeds of the land?" (Acts 5:1–3 ESV)*

Let's keep in mind this is under grace and in a giving scenario. That is how serious His presence inside you is. God doesn't live in that ark anymore; He lives in us.

When you realize God lives in you and is with you twenty-four hours a day, seven days a week, you will live differently. To the measure you love Him and obey His commands is the measure He makes His home in you. As He makes his home in you, you become more like Him.

> *Jesus answered him, "If anyone loves me, he will keep my word, and my Father will love him, and we will come to him and make our home with him." (John 14:23 ESV)*

> *By this is love perfected with us, so that we*
> *may have confidence for the day of judgment,*
> *because as he is so also are we in this world. (1*
> *John 4:17 ESV)*

A few years ago, the Lord gave me an idea for a T-shirt with the words "I Am in me" on the front. He knows I'm always looking for an opportunity to share the gospel with others. The Word says:

> *So we are Christ's ambassadors; God is*
> *making his appeal through us. We speak for*
> *Christ when we plead, "Come back to God!" (2*
> *Corinthians 5:20 NLT)*

I am always looking for ways that the Great I Am who resides in this vessel can appeal to others. He said He would attract those He is wooing to be attracted to the shirt and make a comment. I know when someone says anything about the shirt, He wants to talk to them.

I had my landscaping and lawn pest control people come to the house one day. As I was outside and the truck pulled up, I noticed my regular guy had a partner that day. When they pulled up, one of them commented on my shirt. To be honest, I was more concerned with the lawn, so I immediately went to what needed to be done in the yard.

As I walked in my house, I didn't get ten steps inside before I heard the Lord ask me if I was okay. I replied, "Oh, wait, You wanted to talk to them?"

I walked back outside and approached the man and said, "I'm sorry, but when you pulled up, you mentioned the shirt, and I wasn't paying attention. As soon as I went inside, the Lord spoke to me and wanted to talk to you."

Long story short, the Lord was able to minister to them, and I prayed with both of them. The shirt opened the door. My relationship with the Lord showed them how we can live in fellowship with Him.

I will share one more story about the shirt because it has helped open the door for salvations, reality, and healing. One of the women who was coming to our fellowship was quiet as a mouse. I gave her a shirt, however, and encouraged, "I know the scriptures that are listed, and trust me that if anyone comments on the shirt, the Lord will direct your words."

Within a few months, she was at Publix, and a lady chased her down to comment on the shirt. All she could say was, "We are having revival services, and I just got baptized in the Holy Ghost." She was nervous and quickly shared her experience. The lady got her contact info, went to one of the meetings, and received a healing for a blood disease she had in her body. Praise Jesus!

The "I Am in me" concept came from the Lord. It has provided many opportunities for those who are willing to wear the shirts. Moreover, it has helped the person wearing it recognize and believe God is with and in them all the time.

How can I wear this shirt and live as the world lives? When I get the full reality that the Great I Am—who once lived in a box called the ark and was so holy that even a good deed known to man could kill Him—now lives inside of me, I might just live differently. My flesh realizes what my spirit already knows. It is vital in these last days that we know and understand these truths.

> *THEREFORE BE imitators of God [copy Him and follow His example], as well-beloved children [imitate their father]. (Ephesians 5:1 AMPC)*

You see, to be imitators of God, we must go back to Jesus's example. We take God everywhere we go, and if it's a bad situation, we change it like Jesus did. We do not get caught up in it.

> *No soldier when in service gets entangled in the enterprises of [civilian] life; his aim is to satisfy and please the one who enlisted him. (2 Timothy 2:4 AMPC)*

Train your vessel. Paul says:

> *But [like a boxer] I buffet my body [handle it roughly, discipline it by hardships] and subdue it, for fear that after proclaiming to others the Gospel and things pertaining to it, I myself should become unfit [not stand the test, be unapproved and rejected as a counterfeit]. (1 Corinthians 9:27 AMPC)*

What is he training his body to do? To be an imitator of God who is in him. If the outside doesn't match the inside, then he can be called a fake. So do whatever it takes for you to acknowledge, believe, and understand the fact that God lives in you.

Your vessel was created to do the works of God not by religious duty but out of the flow of your intimacy from Him in you.

> *For by grace you have been saved by faith.*
> *Nothing you did could ever earn this salvation,*
> *for it was the love gift from God that brought us*
> *to Christ! So no one will ever be able to boast,*
> *for salvation is never a reward for good works*
> *or human striving. We have become his poetry,*
> *a re-created people that will fulfill the destiny*
> *he has given each of us, for we are joined to*
> *Jesus, the Anointed One. Even before we were*
> *born, God planned in advance our destiny*
> *and the good works we would do to fulfill it!*
> *(Ephesians 2:8–10 TPT)*

No contradiction here. You are not saved by your own ability or works, but the works of Him flow through you. Jesus provided this beauty that speaks to this.

> *I am a true sprouting vine, and the farmer*
> *who tends the vine is my Father. He cares for*
> *the branches connected to me by lifting and*
> *propping up the fruitless branches and pruning*

every fruitful branch to yield a greater harvest. The words I have spoken over you have already cleansed you. So you must remain in life-union with me, for I remain in life-union with you. For as a branch severed from the vine will not bear fruit, so your life will be fruitless unless you live your life intimately joined to mine. "I am the sprouting vine and you're my branches. As you live in union with me as your source, fruitfulness will stream from within you—but when you live separated from me you are powerless. (John 15:1–5 TPT)

In Closing

Maybe you made it through this book and realized your walk with the Lord isn't what it could be (not questioning anyone's salvation). You just realize that there is more available to you in God.

Or maybe you read this book and you've never given your life to God, but you say to yourself, "You know, I want a life where I can hear God's voice. That I can know who created everything. I want a life that He can live and dwell in this vessel, temple, body. I want this new life." The scriptures say:

> *If you openly declare that Jesus is Lord and believe in your heart that God raised him from the dead, you will be saved. For it is by believing in your heart that you are made right with God, and it is by openly declaring your faith that you are saved. (Romans 10:9–10 NLT)*

"Believing in your heart" has been addressed in this book with several examples. It is a new life, a new creation in Christ; old things have passed away, so don't go back to them. Repentance means turning from the old ways.

> *Therefore if any person is [ingrafted] in*
> *Christ (the Messiah) he is a new creation (a*
> *new creature altogether); the old [previous*
> *moral and spiritual condition] has passed*
> *away. Behold, the fresh and new has come! (2*
> *Corinthians 5:17 AMPC)*

True belief is a surrender to and falling in love with Jesus. When you surrender your heart to your spouse, they are the one and only. There is no one else who should even come close to them. They have your whole heart, and your marriage thrives because of your passion, love, and discipline to them.

It's time to turn your attention to Him and talk to Him. Pray this earnestly with your heart out loud and desire a walk with God as Adam did before sin:

> *Father, I read this book. This man seems*
> *to know You in a way that I know not of. He*
> *has a passion that I would like. A friendship*
> *and relationship with You I desire. Forgive me*
> *for my sin. Forgive me for not inviting You into*
> *all of my life. I surrender to You. I surrender*
> *everything to You. I give You everything that*
> *I have. I empty myself of this life and ask that*
> *You come, Holy Spirit, and fill me. Fill me that*
> *I may overflow Your life in me to others. Spirit*
> *of Jesus, come into my life, live in this temple,*

and fulfill the good work You created me for.
Thank You, Jesus.

Father, I thank You that you've heard their call. You've heard their heart. You've heard their desires. So I thank You that You will fill them with Your own Spirit in order to empower them to live according to Your way and Your will. As Ezekiel prophesied:

> *And I will put my Spirit within you and*
> *cause you to walk in My statutes, and you shall*
> *heed My ordinances and do them. (Ezekiel*
> *36:27 AMPC)*

So I thank You that You fill them with Your Holy Spirit and touch them. This very day, I break every hindrance off of them, every relationship that is contrary to fulfilling their mission, their purpose You created them for. I break it off now. In Jesus's name. Relationships go! Hindrances go! Thank You, Jesus!

Do you need healing in your body? I command healing to your body with full restoration of your physical and mental health. Be released from your torment this day in Jesus's name!

Father, I thank You for empowering them by Your grace, cascading Your love and mercy over them all the days of their lives.

About the Author

Leonardo Gomez has been a steadfast Christian for twenty-seven years. During that time, he led street evangelism, helped in youth ministry, and worked with troubled teens in a juvenile detention center.

In 2016, following a Word from God, Leonardo left the corporate world after eighteen years, to step into full-time ministry, launching Xtreme Agape. The ministry's main focus is hearing God for yourself through reading the Word, discipling men, and helping marriages thrive.

Leonardo is a devoted husband and father and has been married to his wife, Amy, for twenty years. They have five kids and two grandchildren. He is a first-generation American from Cuba and resides in Central Florida with his wife.